IMAGES
of America

# PIERCE COUNTY

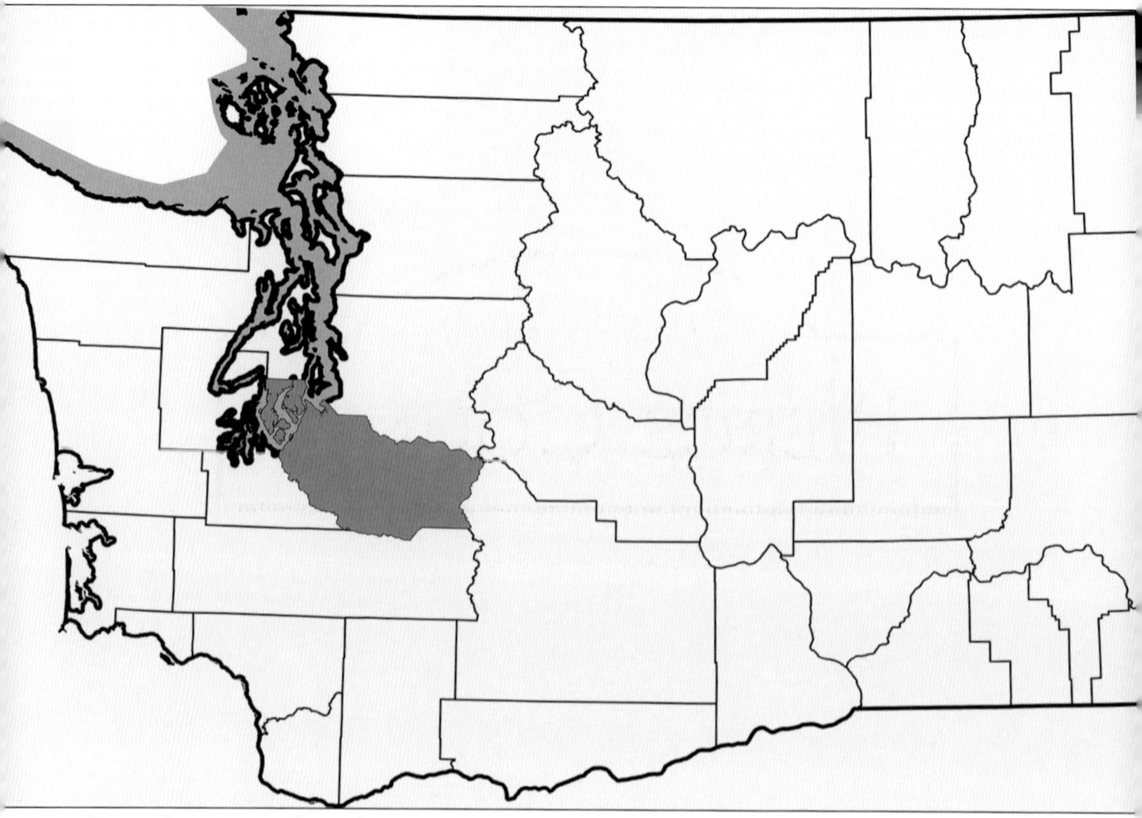

Pierce County is indicated in gray on this map, showing its location in western Washington at the southern end of Puget Sound. Pierce County includes the entirety of Mount Rainier National Park. (Courtesy David Benbennick.)

**ON THE COVER:** These 12 Daffodil Festival princesses are gathered in the Chervenka family daffodil farm on the east side of the Sumner-Orting Highway. Standing from left to right are Sandra Lilyblad, of Sumner; Lani Torre, of Wilson High School; Chris Rupp, of Sumner; Julie Wahlgren, of Stadium High School; Caryn Chervenka, of Puyallup; Sally Yoder, of Sumner; Shelia Keogan, of Puyallup; Jo Anne Tatum, of Clover Park High School; Gail Christenson, of Puyallup; Anita Johnson, of Lincoln High School; and Gail Eagan, of Orting. Kneeling in front is Carol Mill of Franklin Pierce High School, who was the reigning Daffodil queen in 1959. This photograph was taken on March 19, 1959, by Richards Studio. (Courtesy Tacoma Public Library.)

IMAGES
*of America*

# PIERCE COUNTY

Donald R. Tjossem

ARCADIA
PUBLISHING

ISBN 978-1-4671-0476-0

Published by Arcadia Publishing
Charleston, South Carolina

Printed in the United States of America

Library of Congress Control Number: 2019950722

For all general information, please contact Arcadia Publishing:
Telephone 843-853-2070
Fax 843-853-0044
E-mail sales@arcadiapublishing.com
For customer service and orders:
Toll-Free 1-888-313-2665

Visit us on the Internet at www.arcadiapublishing.com

*To all the dedicated photographers who have recorded and documented these historical images of Pierce County for all to enjoy.*

# Contents

# Acknowledgments

This book is dedicated to all the photographers in Pierce County who made these images and to all personnel, past and present, in the Northwest Room at the Tacoma Public Library who have very carefully catalogued and described these images for the public to enjoy. This would include Brian Kamens and Ilona Perry, who were very helpful with the publication of this book.

My wife, Becky Alexander, has been of major assistance and support in producing this book as she edits and reviews my writing. She makes my writing appear much better than it really is.

Arcadia Publishing always has helpful staff who are invaluable in the production of a book such as this. I would like to acknowledge Erin Vosgien, acquisitions editor; Caroline Anderson, title manager; and Jim Kempert, Senior Production Editor, who have been of great assistance in producing this book.

Unless otherwise noted, all images are from the Northwest Room of the Tacoma Public Library.

# Introduction

Pierce County was formed by the legislature of the Oregon Territory on December 22, 1852. Before that time, it was part of Thurston County. Its namesake, Franklin Pierce, was the 14th president of the United States, from March 4, 1853, to March 4, 1857. When Washington was made a state on November 11, 1889, Pierce County was included as one of its original 39 counties.

Mount Rainier is Pierce County's most notable landmark, being the tallest mountain and volcano in the Cascade Range at 14,410 feet in elevation. Its last major eruption was about 1,000 years ago. Approximately 10,000 people attempt to climb it each year, and about half are successful. Only trained climbers should attempt this feat.

Puget Sound, which is often called the Salish Sea by the indigenous peoples, is another distinctive and unique feature of Pierce County and is an inlet of the Pacific Ocean. This gives Pierce County the distinction of having a glaciated mountain and deepwater ocean access within its boundaries.

When Pierce County was first set aside by the Oregon Territory, the population stood at about 1,000. By the time Washington became a state in 1889, the population was approximately 50,000. Following the announcement that the Northern Pacific Railway had named Tacoma the western terminus of its transcontinental railroad, the population grew swiftly.

Pierce County presently has a population approaching 900,000, according to the 2010 US Census, and continues a growth trend that started at its inception. There are plenty of rural areas to allow for growth with easy access to SeaTac International Airport, the Interstate 5 highway corridor, and the deep seaports leading to the Pacific Ocean.

Joint Base Lewis McChord (JBLM) is the county's largest employer, with 53,000 full-time equivalents, followed by MultiCare with 7,700, the State of Washington with 7,600, CHI Franciscan with 6,700, and the City of Tacoma and Tacoma Public Utilities with 3,500. Small businesses and rural farmers make up much of the remaining employers outside of the county seat of Tacoma.

The county adopted and is governed by a charter. There are seven county council members, each from an equally populated district. The council members serve four-year terms. There are parts of four US congressional districts in Pierce County.

Pierce County is home to 16 public school districts and six private schools. There are five university campuses, two public community colleges, and two technical colleges.

Farming has remained an important part of the Pierce County economy with over 45,000 acres still in production. Pierce County leads the United States in rhubarb production, raising about 50 percent of the US supply. The Puyallup Valley's farmers also lead the state in producing lettuce, cabbage, radishes, and green onions. The county leads the state some years in pumpkin production. Tulips and daffodils are also significant crops in the county.

The value of the 80 agricultural crops, livestock, and livestock products is $80 million, which ranks Pierce 14th among the state's 39 counties. The county's agricultural base is shrinking, though, as farmers and farmland are lost to urbanization.

Typical summer afternoon temperatures range from the 70s to the low 80s, with average winter temperatures in the 40s. Summer afternoon winds ranging from 0 to 15 miles per hour are ideal for sailing on the plentiful waters in Pierce County. Winter temperatures seldom drop below freezing, and snow is not guaranteed every year at the lower levels.

The Puyallup Indians have lived in villages from the foothills of Mount Rainier along the rivers and creeks to the shores of Puget Sound for thousands of years. Their villages were scattered throughout the many islands, prairies, and rich valley country of the Pacific Northwest. Native American historians often noted that because of the abundance of salmon and shellfish, "when the tides were out, the table was spread."

Pierce County is very mindful and active regarding its history, with the Washington State History Museum taking a prominent place on Pacific Avenue, the main street in Tacoma. This is supplemented by many city and local museums throughout the county. There are also many specialty arts and culture museums that relate to local history.

In 1946, the Pierce County Library System, with seven branches, served 55,000 people. Today, Pierce County Library is the state's fourth-largest library system, with 19 libraries serving 602,000 people. Significant growth in the library systems has been shown since 1946, when the Pierce County Library offered 6,385 books. Today, the Pierce County Library System offers 1.5 million books, CDs, DVDs, and audiobooks. It also offers computers with high-speed Internet access and free Wi-Fi.

# *One*

# North

## Fife, Milton, and Brown's Point

The Zebra Fireworks stand was a very popular place in Milton on July 3, 1953. This photograph shows eager Pierce County and King County residents purchasing firecrackers, sparklers, and other pyrotechnics. Even though fireworks were banned in both Pierce and King County at this time, the laws did not apply to the city of Milton.

In June 1939, Oscar V. Brown stands at the Brown's Point Lighthouse. He was a longtime lighthouse keeper and had been with the lighthouse since 1903. This was the second lighthouse at Brown's Point, which the US Coast Guard built in 1934. Brown retired on November 1, 1939.

Shirley Jackson is signing the register at Brown's Point Lighthouse while her friend Anita Rowe awaits her turn. This photograph was taken on June 14, 1939, while Oscar V. Brown, for whom the lighthouse was named, looks on. Brown was the keeper at the lighthouse until he retired at age 70.

This 1942 photograph shows the Sound View Mobil gas station at Brown's Point. When a car pulled up to the station for a fill-up in those days, an attendant would pump the gas and wash the windows as part of the service at the service station.

From left to right are Bill Taylor, Virginia Judd, Bob Almvig, Ann Louise Greiwe, and Richard Cummings as they register for classes during Freshman Week at the College of Puget Sound on September 19, 1939. They are posing with the old fog bell from Brown's Point Lighthouse. A captain of the Lighthouse Service, Oscar V. Brown donated the bell to the college when the lighthouse was modernized and the new automatic fog signal was installed.

Nelson Bennett (October 14, 1843–July 22, 1913) was a past president of Metro Parks, owned the *Tacoma Ledger* newspaper and the Hotel Bennett, and contracted to build railroad tunnels in Tacoma. This pioneer, who was originally born in Canada, had many interests, among them developing the town of Fairhaven near Bellingham. His last project was the Nelson Bennett Tunnel, shown below, just south of Point Defiance Park. Salmon Beach houses can be seen at left. Bennett died on the eve of the completion of this tunnel, which is still in use today.

This photograph shows both the American Smelting and Refining Company smokestack before it was blown up on January 17, 1993, and the Northern Pacific tracks emerging out of the Nelson Bennett Tunnel on the west side of Point Defiance Park. The other end of the tunnel is shown on the opposite page. The tunnel is 4,000 feet in length.

In 1941, the Fife High School basketball team won the league championship with a record of 11-1. The team, pictured on February 24, 1941, consisted of, from left to right, (first row) Yahachi Sagami, Bob Vinson, Roy Herting, Frank Dreyer, Dave Wilcox, and Coach Bill Vinson; (second row) Willard Ogden, Bill Haminshi, Frank Spear, Mel Rowe, and Frank Evancich.

This photograph of the Poodle Dog in Fife was taken on October 6, 1949. This landmark restaurant originally opened as a hamburger stand in 1933. This structure was replaced by the current building in 1967.

The Century Ballroom was in Fife, near the Poodle Dog restaurant. Built by Rocco "Mac" Manza and Emilio James "Jimmy" Zarelli in 1934, it was the venue for such famous bands as the Dorsey Brothers, Duke Ellington, Guy Lombardo, and Nat King Cole. In the 1950s, big bands were replaced by rock and roll, and the ballroom was closed and redeveloped as a retail space. It burned down in 1956.

Blanche Cerino, left, and Elizabeth Thomas are holding a publicity poster for the Firemen's Ball, which was to be held at the Century Ballroom on November 20, 1935. The dance was to sponsor the Northwest Fire College the next year. Attending would be firefighters and officials from Washington, Oregon, Idaho, Montana, and Canada to exchange ideas and instructions on firefighting.

Kameo Kajimura is shown cutting celery for the western Washington market on his 20-acre farm in Fife. He planted three acres of celery but had to eventually discontinue growing it as California growers were able to ship celery much cheaper than he could. The celery season ran from September until frost hit the Fife area.

Hareo Kajimura, son of Kameo Kajimura, is holding large bunches of celery, which would be marketed to restaurants in the area. The celery bunches were placed in crates, 20 per bunch. The two photographs on this page were taken on October 28, 1962.

This photograph, taken on December 17, 1948, shows the four main buildings of the Fife School District No. 88 on Twentieth Street East, just east of Fifty-fifth Avenue East. From left to right are Fife High School, which was constructed in 1930; Fife Civic Auditorium, built in 1924; the old Fife School, which was raised in 1914; and Fife Elementary School, which was built in 1936. A newer high school was built in 1949 and dedicated in 1950, but has now been replaced.

On November 12, 1938, the four women on the right are ready to perform a traditional Japanese dance at the Fife High School for the Japanese American Citizen's League's annual carnival and bazaar. The dancers are, from left to right, Betty Sasaki, Dorothy Norisada, Miyo Yoshida, and Amy Marumoto. On the left are Haruko Yaguchi (standing), Fugiye Sasaki (seated), Lillian Mizukami (kneeling), and three-year-old Arlene Sakahara.

Pictured is the Dash Point School, which was built in 1924. By 1974, it was closed due to lack of enrollment but was reopened four years later and remained open until 1993. On December 2, 1996, it was placed in the Washington Heritage Register.

From left to right, Cub Scouts Tommy Thompson, Thomas Gallagher, Jerry Lerum, and Benny Gallagher stop Andrew Anderson and his wife as they were driving through northeast Tacoma to hand them a flier advertising the 12th annual Dash Point Dock dinner. The dinner was held on Saturday, July 23, 1938, at the Dash Point Dock, followed by a dance at the Dash Point Community Hall at 9:00 p.m.

On June 1, 1938, these geoduck diggers were successful in their efforts during a low tide at Dash Point. From left to right are Delores Koval, age 8; Donny Koval, age 2 ½; and Dorothy Tomchick, age 15, holding the shovel they used.

The Sea-Tac Shipyard All-Stars are shown on March 14, 1943, at the Tacoma Boys Club. They were a Pierce County Inter-League basketball team sponsored by the Seattle Tacoma Shipbuilding Corporation. From left to right are (first row) Vic Lyon, Frank Ferrians, Verne Goodwin, Pete Hilt, Phil Red Eagle, Bob Ness, and Pat Piper; (second row) Ron Ferrians, Ernie Bighorn, Mason Longmire (manager), Dip Loveland, Clarence Gottgetreu, and Stan Buckhalter.

# *Two*

# South

## Steilacoom, Joint Base Lewis McChord, Graham, and Orting

This 1885 photograph shows the Steilacoom Transfer Company, located at the corner of Wilkes and Commercial Streets. Nick Doering owned this firm, which was one of Steilacoom's oldest businesses. His son and grandson operated it from after his death in 1942 until it was sold in 1971 to the Lakewood Fuel Company.

This young boy is watching a man playing the tuba for the Steilacoom Band. The Steilacoom Band would be playing for the upcoming Steilacoom Music Festival in 1936.

The entire Steilacoom Band is posing in front of the town hall after a practice session for the upcoming Steilacoom Music Festival on August 2, 1936. This festival was hosted by local veterans' groups and attended by thousands of visitors. A loudspeaker system was used to carry the music over several miles.

C.L. Whitney is shown at the east end of Wagon Bridge over Steilacoom Lake. He was a driver for the Hill Hardware Company, located in the 2300 block of Pacific Avenue in Tacoma. This photograph was taken around 1908.

On July 12, 1962, this German Amphicar was tested in American Lake. There were 3,878 of these cars built in Germany between 1961 and 1968. In the water, they had a speed of seven miles per hour. On the highway, they could reach 70 miles per hour. Richard Clemens and Buddy How are fishing from the back seat, and Douglas Stubblefield is in the front seat with the unidentified driver.

This photograph shows two Steilacoom School District No. 1 buildings in 1916. The brick building in front had just been completed at a cost $15,000. The wooden building behind it was originally constructed in 1892 and was torn down in 1917.

Gretchen Kunigk Fraser won both a gold and silver medal in skiing events at the 1948 Winter Olympics in St. Moritz, Switzerland. Her parents, Clara and Willibald A. Kunigk, are shown with her riding in the April 1948 Daffodil Parade. Fraser was the first American to win an Olympic gold medal in skiing. Much of her initial training was done on the rope tow at Mount Rainier. Willibald Kunigk was the City of Tacoma water superintendent when he retired in 1956 after 39 years.

In the summer of 1925, these National Bank of Tacoma employees held an annual party at what was the DeKoven Inn, which was on the east side of Lake Steilacoom. The inn was destroyed by a fire on August 2 of that year, although its banquet and dance hall were saved and eventually became a new inn after much of the property was subdivided and sold.

In July 1927, Harry Thessen, left, and Charles "Mac" MacLaughlin are standing by the service cars of the Tacoma Gas & Fuel Company. Thessen served the south end of Tacoma, and MacLaughlin served the north end. They installed meters and investigated leaks and gas appliance problems as well as other service calls.

The Oaks, on Lake Steilacoom, is pictured in this 1924 photograph. It offered bathing, boating, picnic grounds, and dancing. It also had a long slide that included a platform diving tower. This facility was used for the 1924 Olympic swimming trials. It later was called The Towers, and in 1938, it was converted to the Lakewood Ice Arena before being demolished in 1982 for the development of lakefront condominiums.

It took Jackie Myers of Orting half an hour to land the 21-pound steelhead trout at left on February 2, 1947. Using a 7.5-ounce rod with 12-pound test nylon line, this was a pretty good feat for a person who only weighed 95 pounds and stood five feet tall. Myers was competing in a *Tacoma Times* and Washington Sports Shop fishing derby on the Hoh River.

This monument was erected in downtown Steilacoom to commemorate the first Protestant church to be built north of the Columbia River in 1853. The monument was built by the congregation of Rev. John F. DeVore on the site of the church and includes the original church bell.

This is the Bair drug and hardware store as is appeared shortly after being built in 1895 by pharmacist Warren L. Bair; it was a drugstore at the time. This store was eventually donated to the Steilacoom Historical Museum Association in 1973 by Eudocia Bair Leech and Godfrey "Cub" Bair. It is now operated as The Bistro and is a working museum.

This is what the front of the main Western State Hospital building looked like on October 12, 1921, before the present one was built. Today, the hospital has more than 800 patient beds and 2,200 employees to care for the mentally ill and is the regional state psychiatric hospital for 20 western Washington counties.

On March 30, 1938, the Pierce County Airport became obsolete as county officials signed a deed for 900 acres, including the Tacoma field with buildings, to the US War Department. This facility then became known as McChord Field, which is now part of Joint Base Lewis McChord (JBLM). John Schlarb, seated at left, was chairman of the board of Pierce County Commissioners. Seated at right is County Commissioner Alexander Rankin. Standing are, from left to right, Col. Frank W. Wright, commander of the new airbase; Clifford Davis, county auditor; Commissioner Guy Melton; Frank Walsh, industrial engineer of the Tacoma Chamber of Commerce; and Wilbur Raleigh.

Gen. Dwight D. Eisenhower, center, exits an automobile while on a visit to Fort Lewis in 1942. This photograph was taken by the *Fort Lewis Sentinel* while General Eisenhower was attending an American Legion convention, held from August 20 to August 22. Eisenhower was appointed commanding general of the European theater in June 1942 and eventually served two terms, from 1953 to 1961, as the 34th president of the United States. He passed away on March 28, 1969.

William Mueller is lifting a netful of humpback salmon from a trap at a state salmon hatchery at Voight's Creek near Orting. Helping Mueller is Clarence Duncan, superintendent of the hatchery, on October 21, 1937.

This 1937 photograph shows an overall view of the hatchery at that time. Voight's Creek, off the Puyallup River, is one of seven fish hatcheries in Pierce County.

This photograph, taken on May 23, 1927, shows the ferry used on the most direct route from Filucy Bay in Longbranch, on the Key Peninsula, to Steilacoom. The ferry ran from 1924 until 1954 on the southern end of Puget Sound carrying passengers and automobiles and included stops at Anderson Island. It was built by the Washington Navigation Company in the Skansie Shipyard at Gig Harbor.

Charles Turner was a bullfrog farmer in Steilacoom, as shown in this photograph taken on July 30, 1937. At the time, he had over 50,000 frogs, which he raised and sent to market as the delicacy frog legs. Turner had four frog ponds in which to rear the frogs, which took about three years to reach the marketable size of 30–36 inches.

USS *Shenandoah* was the first of four US Navy rigid airships. Constructed between 1922 and 1923 at Lakehurst Naval Air Station, it is shown here at Camp Lewis in October 1924. The special mooring mast at left was constructed for this visit. Nine months later, on September 3, 1925, the airship was torn to pieces in Ohio when it was caught in a thunderstorm. Twenty-nine of its 43 crew members survived the crash.

In the summer of 1945, over 50,000 soldiers were scheduled to be stationed at Fort Lewis, as it was the headquarters of the 3rd Infantry Division. This is a partial view of the barracks and buildings at that time, just prior to World War II.

This photograph was taken around 1900 in Steilacoom at the end of the electric streetcar line. The Tacoma and Steilacoom Railway Company started in 1890. At that time, it was the world's first interurban streetcar system and ran 12 miles from Tacoma through University Place and Chambers Creek on its way to Steilacoom.

In January 1956, the members of the Pacific Lutheran College Choir of the West posed in the form of a cross with Prof. Gunnar Malmin, director, standing at the base. This choir toured the Pacific coast states for an annual two-week period with a sacred music program. On this tour, the choir gave various concerts, including to prison inmates, and appeared on radio broadcasts.

This is Nathaniel Orr's Wagon Shop in Steilacoom as it appeared around 1880. Orr also made other items such as beds, tables, chairs, spinning wheels, and coffins. In addition, he had an operating orchard in town. The Steilacoom Historical Museum Association (SHMA) purchased Orr's home and orchard and placed it in the Washington Heritage Register and National Register of Historic Places. The building is now open during special events in Steilacoom, by special request, or during normal museum hours.

On February 24, 1922, these 10 communication specialists from Camp Lewis stood before their large truck that contained a wireless telephone and radio system with Magnavox speakers. This team was able to hear daily news and music from as far away as San Francisco and weather reports from ships far out at sea. They also broadcast music from military bands as far as their transmitter would reach.

The Civilian Conservation Corps (CCC) had 29 camps in March 1941. This boy is receiving training in one of its radio rooms, complete with a transmitter, at Camp Electron, Pierce County. Between 1933 and 1942, the CCC also trained young men in welding, blacksmithing, plumbing, and road construction.

Gov. Clarence D. Martin shakes the hand of Gerald K. Kelley, who received the Order of the Rose medal on August 3, 1938, for being the most soldierly, patriotic, and meritorious participant of a Citizens Military Camp held at Fort Lewis, when 250 young men attended a military training program there. Martin was the 11th governor of Washington, the first to be born in the state. He served two terms, from 1933 to 1941.

On March 29, 1927, cameraman Arthur Edeson of First National Productions is shown filming *The Patent Leather Kit*. It was filmed on the grounds of Camp (Fort) Lewis. Edeson was also the cameraman for other films, such as *Mutiny on the Bounty*, *All Quiet on the Western Front*, and *Casablanca*. It was not unusual for movies to be filmed at Camp Lewis at this time.

Twin sisters Lucia Rose Rigney O'Donnell, left, and Marcelle Catherine Rigney Henly were born in 1862. They were the second set of twins born to John and Elizabeth Rigney, who arrived in Washington Territory in 1849 as a military couple assigned to Fort Steilacoom. The sisters taught school and operated the area's first Western Union telegraph in Steilacoom. They lived together at the Rigney home in Steilacoom after becoming widows and were record keepers for Western State Hospital until 1950.

An E.I. DuPont de Nemours & Co. official is at the podium for the celebration of the 50-year anniversary of the DuPont plant in Pierce County on August 29, 1959. Since the plant's beginning in 1909, over one billion pounds of explosives had been produced, according to management at that time. This area was not normally open to visitors, and all matches, cigarettes, and lighters were confiscated before anyone could attend the ceremony.

Johnny Wray was a resident at the soldiers' home in Orting when this photograph was taken on February 12, 1936. He was 92 years old. He stated he could remember being rebuked by President Lincoln in Illinois for running away from home to join the Union army in the Civil War when he was only 17 years old. At the time this photograph was taken, he had nine living children, three of whom, all daughters, lived in Pierce County. Wray passed away on October 18, 1937, at the soldiers' home.

The State Bank of Buckley originally opened in 1920. This photograph shows what it looked like in 1937, after renovations in 1930. In an attempted bank robbery on July 1, 1925, two bandits were killed in the streets of Buckley, and William Rose, one of the city's merchants, who was defending the bank, died the next day from a gunshot wound. Today, the bank still looks as it did in this photograph, although it is empty.

# *Three*

# Central Tacoma

This view of Pacific Avenue facing north was taken on January 25, 1939. It shows Hotel Lewis on the left and Hotel Croft at right, which was owned by Lee Croft, who later became Pierce County sheriff. On the right can be seen the Puget Sound National Bank building. Note the streetcar tracks in the road, which were still in use at the time.

In March 1934, this German cruiser, the *Karlsruhe*, was taking on fuel from a Foss barge in Commencement Bay. While this ship was in port, over 4,700 people went aboard on March 18 for a tour. The *Karlsruhe* was later sunk by the British when Germany invaded Norway on April 9, 1940.

Machinist Mate Carl Lischke is being laid to rest at Mountain View Memorial Park on March 19, 1939, with his six German shipmates as pallbearers for the ceremony. Lischke died from fish poisoning from fish eaten on the cruiser *Karlsruhe*. Many shipmates and Tacoma citizens attended the services.

Construction started in 1919 for the Scandinavian American Bank, but the bank failed in 1921 before the building was completed. On June 25, 1925, it opened as the home of the Washington-California Company. It has been known both as the Bank of California Building and the Washington Building. It was the second-highest structure in the entire Northwest, at 17 stories and 237 feet, when it was completed.

Celebrating his 49th birthday while visiting Tacoma in support of a World War II bond drive is William Harrison "Jack" Dempsey, who was born on June 24, 1895. Dempsey was heavyweight champion of the world from 1919 to 1926, and when this photograph was taken on June 24, 1944, he was a lieutenant commander in the US Coast Guard.

On January 25, 1922, the four-masted steel sailing ship *William T. Lewis* was berthed at Terminal Dock in Tacoma unloading nitrates from South America. Capt. N.P. Carlson was the commander of this 30-year-old bark, which had survived an attack by a German submarine during World War I.

The ground-breaking ceremony for the Tacoma Dome took place on July 1, 1981. This structure was partially made of fallen timber from the 1980 Mount St. Helens volcanic eruption. The Tacoma Dome is the largest indoor venue in the state of Washington. It is 530 feet in diameter and 152 feet tall, can accommodate up to 23,000 patrons, and is owned and operated by the City of Tacoma's venues and events department.

Wade H. Perrow Sr. is displaying his skiing trophy at Stadium High School. Perrow was selected as the outstanding individual performer for 1939 at the College of Puget Sound (now university). Perrow was born on April 9, 1920, and passed away on August 17, 1988. His son Wade H. Perrow Jr. was the founder of Wade Perrow Construction, which is based in Gig Harbor.

Tacoma mayor Joseph J. Kaufman (left) greets Louise and Bob Lynd on December 20, 1939, as they step off the train at Union Station. The Lynds had just completed a six-month trip by Willits canoe down the Mississippi River from Fort Benton, Montana, to New Orleans, Louisiana, to promote Washington's Golden Jubilee. The chairman of the Golden Jubliee, Harry P. Cain, is at right. The celebration had sponsored the 3,500-mile journey, which in part retraced the path of the Lewis and Clark expedition. The Lynds wrote a series of articles relating their experiences to publicize the Golden Jubilee.

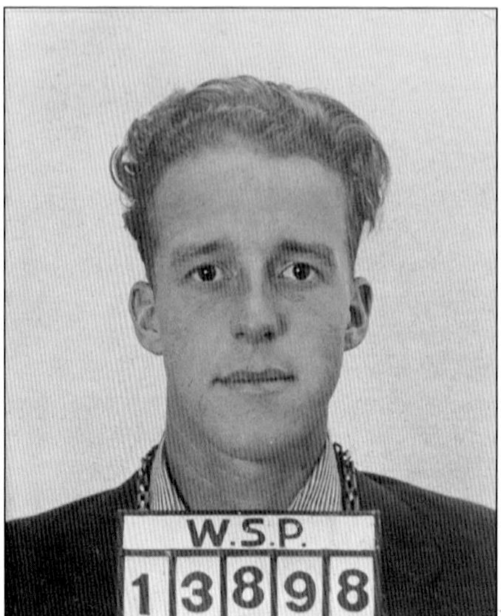


On May 24, 1935, Harmon Metz Waley from Puyallup kidnapped George H. Weyerhaeuser, who was nine years old at the time and the son of a prominent businessman, J.P. Weyerhaeuser. George was released by Waley after the $200,000 ransom was paid on June 1, 1935, near Issaquah, Washington. Waley was sentenced to 45 years in prison but was paroled from the US penitentiary on Alcatraz Island on June 3, 1963, at the age of 52, after serving approximately 28 years. Waley wrote to his victim from prison on several occasions, apologizing for his actions. When he was released, he asked for a job. In a demonstration of compassion, George Weyerhaeuser found a job for Waley at one of his Oregon plants.

From 1982 to 1989, Doug Sutherland served as the mayor of Tacoma for two terms, while also owning Tacoma Tent and Awning Company. Sutherland later served as Pierce County executive from January 1993 to December 2000. Following that, he was elected to be commissioner of public lands for the state of Washington, an office he held from 2001 through 2009.

In front of Manley Motors are, from left to right, James Teale, driver of the Daimler-Knight limousine shown in front; Harry Manley, president of Manley Motors; Captain Gardner, of the Tacoma Police Department, at the wheel of the Willys-Knight 70 sedan; police chief Marvin D. Guy; and Joe Willits, shop superintendent of Manley Motors. The four men in the doorway are unidentified.

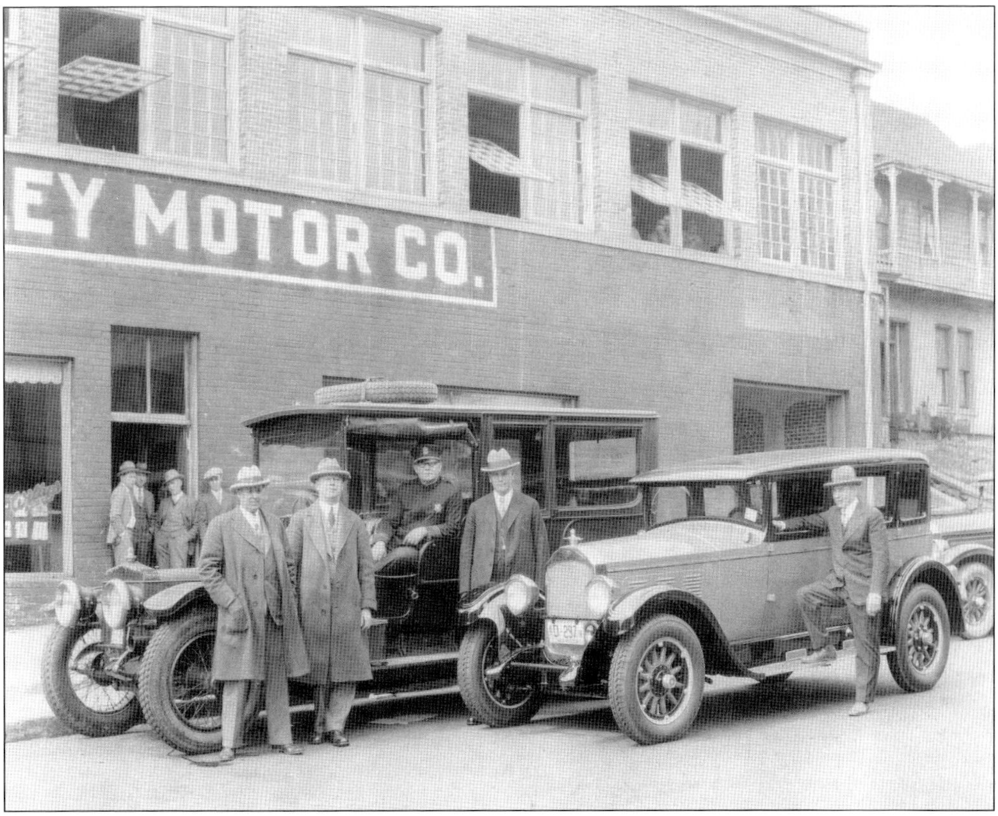

April 8, 1933, was declared "Roosevelt Day" by Mayor Melvin G. Tennent and the Tacoma City Council to recognize Pres. Franklin D. Roosevelt's leadership during the country's economic crisis in the Great Depression. This photograph shows a truck advertising Carstens, which was a large meatpacking firm in Tacoma at the time.

On February 26, 1936, these men are pushing wheelbarrows full of dirt on a Works Progress Administration (WPA) project under the direction of F.A. Halveson, at far right in the dark jacket and boots. This gravel road project was for a section of South Tyler Street from Snake Lake to South Sixty-sixth Street. The WPA was a federal relief program created by President Roosevelt that employed millions during the Depression.

This photograph of Mamie Jacobs was taken on June 28, 1949. She was soon to be installed as the president of the Tacoma Zonta Club. In October 1949, the club observed its 21st anniversary. Jacobs retired after 49 years with Pacific Telephone & Telegraph Company and passed away on December 24, 1960.

Jane Hatfield, an employee of the Washington Hardware Company, poses on October 4, 1938, with four black-tailed deer that had been entered in the store's bird and big game hunting contest. The hunters who entered these deer were Richard Hofto, E.R. Howell, Emery Kiske, and James Johnston Jr., all from Orting.

The Washington State College (now university) Cougars played the Texas A&M Aggies in the Evergreen Bowl at Tacoma Stadium on December 6, 1941, the day before the Japanese attacked Pearl Harbor. The Washington State Alumni Association acquired two cougars and paraded them through the streets of Tacoma to build up interest in the game. The Aggies, Southwest Conference champs, defeated the Cougars 7-0 in Tacoma's first experience with big-time college football. The game was attended by an estimated 30,000 people.

Jacqueline Noel served as Tacoma city librarian from 1924 until her retirement in 1947. She had started working in the reference department in 1914. Noel deserves much of the credit for raising funds for the McCormick Branch (now Wheelock) and the Mottet Branch libraries, constructed entirely from citizen donations, which were used for both land and the buildings. She passed away on May 19, 1964.

The Pierce County "Dry Squad" is pictured here. From left to right are Theodore Mohrbacher, Joe Desmond, and Jack Bodaylea. They would confiscate stills and bring them to the old county courthouse until they could be converted into junk by jail trustees. The 18th Amendment, also known as the National Prohibition Act or the Volstead Act, went into effect on October 28, 1919.

On October 23, 1930, Sheriff Tom Desmond is shown with part of a $12,000 still in the county courthouse. The entire still, which could produce 250 gallons of grain alcohol a day, was acquired from a raid at Point Fosdick a few days previous.

Sen. Henry M. Jackson is shown shaking hands with Evan "Skip" Davies, a Democrat candidate for Pierce County sheriff, on September 22, 1970. Davies was receiving the American Federation of Police Honor Award after serving 30 years in law enforcement. The incumbent, Sheriff Carl Petersen, retained his post in this election, winning by approximately 11,000 votes.

The first lumber plant in New Tacoma was the Hatch Mill, which began operations on January 17, 1887. It was owned by Miles F. Hatch and located near what is now 400 Schuster Parkway. The mill was eventually closed in 1887, sold to the Northern Pacific Railway, and dismantled in 1898.

This c. 1889 photograph was taken from the southeast side of Tacoma, the Hawthorne area. The tideflats are in sight, and roads and houses are replacing the former timberlands. The Tacoma Dome would appear at center right nearly 100 years later.

Norman "Benny" Behnke is shown on April 19, 1964, holding a 102-pound octopus he had just pulled out of Puget Sound. He captured this octopus at a depth of 40 feet by jamming its breathing vent until it suffocated. The eighth annual World's Championship Octopus Grapple was held off Titlow Beach on this date.

The photograph above was taken around 1892, while the original Pierce County Court House was under construction. The stone masons are posed in front of what would become a three-story structure with a 230-foot tower, shown at left. This courthouse would be operational for over 60 years, until it was demolished and replaced by the present courthouse in 1959. In June 1893, Pierce County staff began moving into the Pierce County Court House at 1012 G Street. The photograph at left was taken in 1949, ten years before it was demolished and replaced with the present courthouse. The clock faces on all four sides of the tower were eight feet in diameter.

The childhood home of Harry Lillis Crosby Jr., otherwise known as Bing Crosby, is shown here on North J Street. Crosby was born in Tacoma on May 3, 1903, and lived in this home, which his father built in 1902, until the family moved to Spokane in 1906. The house is presently a private residence. (Author's collection.)

Henry William "Lee" Croft is shown on December 21, 1942, shortly after winning the election for Pierce County sheriff. Croft earned the heavyweight boxing title of Canada and won the Pacific Coast heavyweight and light heavyweight championships during his string of 54 undefeated amateur and professional fights. He was born in 1881 and came to Tacoma in 1902. He passed away on December 14, 1951, at the age of 69.

Tacoma mayor Joseph J. Kaufman is being pinned with a "Buddy Poppy" by Jess Dannen of the American Legion Auxiliary. On May 23, 1939, Mayor Kaufman was the first to buy a poppy during Tacoma's Poppy Days. Paper poppies were made in a Walla Walla hospital by disabled veterans and sold to raise funds for veterans' relief.

In December 1951, the Pierce County Sheriff's Department is shown on the Pierce County Court House steps, including both detectives and patrolmen. Sheriff Henry "William" Lee Croft is in the front row at center.

On May 20, 1942, the Coast Guard directed the Tacoma Fire Department to burn what was called "Hollywood on the Tide Flats." There were about 50 shack homes that had been put together during the Great Depression and were to be burned down to protect the industries on the waterfront. This controlled burn lasted several days.

This 1912 White Motor Company truck with a large barrel is being filled by Griffin Fuel Company employees. At this time, heavy trucks could not travel on county or gravel roads in the spring to stop damage to the roads. This smaller truck was used to deliver oil to rural homes that were previously cut off by this ban.

This .32-caliber Smith & Wesson handgun is being given to William P. Bonney, secretary of the Washington State Historical Society, by Fred E. King, retired revenue officer. The handgun had been turned over to King by Fred C. Dean, a notorious opium smuggler, when he was arrested near Anderson Island on July 18, 1905, after a three-decade crime spree. This photograph was taken on October 30, 1934, as King donated the handgun to the society.

These 10 young boys formed a human pyramid on December 3, 1948, as part of a gym class at Gault Junior High School. The students are, from left right, (bottom row) Gene Montgomery, Floyd James, Curtis Oliver, and Mel Laster; (second row) Elmer Garrison, Bill Fjetland, and Jerry Thorsen; (third row) Leonard Hystead and Gary Rostock; (top) Jerry Richardson. Gault Junior High School closed in 2010 and is presently unoccupied.

Shirley Magarity, wife of C.E. Magarity, is standing on a ladder to measure this cross section of a Douglas fir log that is almost 13 feet in diameter. This photograph was taken on October 10, 1946, when the log stood outside the Northwest Door Company before being moved to the Lakewood Branch of the Pierce County Library in 1965, where it remains to this day.

William Jennings Bryan, the famed orator, visited Tacoma on September 15, 1924. He was at one time a presidential candidate and was the 41st secretary of state under Woodrow Wilson from March 5, 1913, to June 9, 1915. He is shown shaking hands with William R. Lee, Democratic nominee for governor. Robert E. Evans, attorney and president of the newly formed Young People's Democratic Club of Tacoma, is to the right.

Two modern iron lungs are being presented to the Pierce County Hospital on January 21, 1941, by the Tacoma District Council of the Lumber and Sawmill Workers Union. These machines were purchased by members of the 13 local unions who gave $1 each to cover the cost of the $2,000 iron lungs. From left to right are Guy Melton, Dr. Burton Brown, Phillip Garland, Earl Hartley, John Binns, Dr. Norman E. Magnussen, and Genevieve Houston. Iron lungs were used to assist polio patients with breathing.

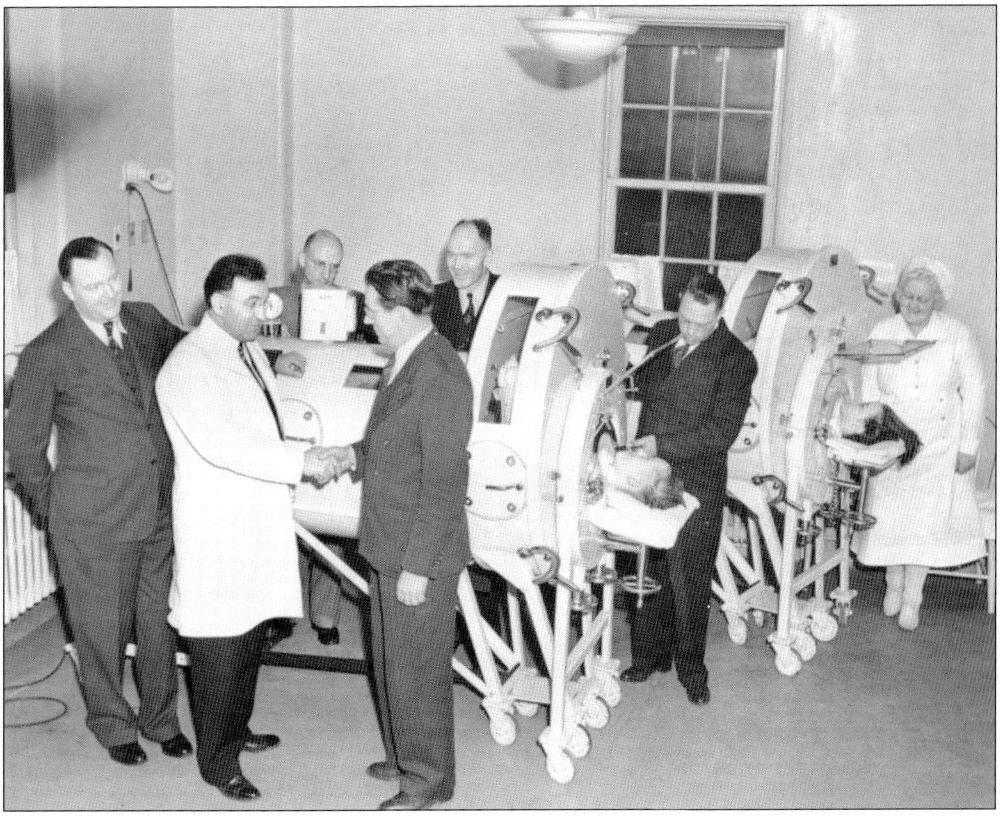

Walter J. Thompson, who owned the Bank of Tacoma and renamed it Merchants National Bank, is shown at left with John S. Baker at the dedication of the new Clover Park Athletic Field. Thompson served on both the territorial legislature in 1886 and the territorial senate. Although he was known as a great philanthropist in the county, the Merchants National Bank failed in the Panic of 1893.

The Fircrest Orthopedic Guild ladies, shown here, sold new 1950 license plates as a fundraiser. From left to right are Mrs. Jack Hawkins, president; Mrs. E.S. Charles, treasurer; and Mrs. Helmut Jueling, vice president and project chairman. The Orthopedic Guilds of Lakewood, Midland, and Fircrest all earned a service fee of 25¢ for each plate sold. If Pierce County residents did not want to pay the 25¢ fee, they could purchase their plates at the county courthouse.

From June 23 to June 28, 1938, the Sons and Daughters of Norway held a convention in Tacoma. This group, which included delegates from Washington, Oregon, California, Idaho, Alaska, and British Columbia, poses in front of Normanna Hall at 1502 South K Street (now Martin Luther King Jr. Way). In 1914, a bazaar was held to start a building fund by the Norway club for Normanna Hall, and after its fundraising efforts were completed, the building was finally dedicated in March 1923. The hall is used today for the Sons of Norway Norden Lodge activities.

From 1936 until 1962, Reno Odlin was president and chief executive officer at Puget Sound National Bank. Odlin was also elected to be the president of the American Bankers Association in 1965 and served a term as director of the Federal Reserve Bank's San Francisco branch. He passed away on September 15, 1979, at the age of 82.

The first branch of Puget Sound National Bank opened in 1895. This photograph, taken on October 10, 1947, shows the Lincoln Branch. On January 15, 1993, Puget Sound National Bank, with 92 branches and $3.1 billion in deposits, was bought out by Key Bank of Cleveland, Ohio.

# *Four*

# East

## Mount Rainier and Puyallup

At an elevation of 6,400 feet, Sunrise is the highest point that can be reached by vehicle at Mount Rainier National Park. This photograph from the east side of Mount Rainier was taken by Asahel Curtis on August 24, 1931, to promote the completion of the road to Sunrise that year. The women were affiliated with the Mary Ann Wells School of the Dance in Seattle. (Courtesy Washington State Historical Society.)

This 24-pound, 2-ounce steelhead was caught by Stan "Fuzzy" Elliot on the Green River near Auburn. The trout made him a leader in the *Tacoma Times* and Washington Ports Shop's fishing derby on February 13, 1947. Elliott was a top semipro baseball pitcher in the Puyallup Valley.

On August 21, 1936, the ninth annual Washington Cooperative Association picnic was held in Sumner, and the 4-H Club ice cream stand was a popular place for many of the attendees. Shown here are three Pierce County commissioners. From left to right are A.A. Rankin, John Schlarb, and Harvey Scofield. Serving the ice cream cones to them are, from left to right, Marion McChesney, Elsa Wahlquist, and her sister Edna Wahlquist. Between 2,000 and 3,000 farmers attended the all-day affair.

The Fairfax Bridge, sometimes known as the James R. O'Farrell Bridge, on the Carbon River is shown on December 17, 1921, during dedication ceremonies attended by a large crowd. At the time the bridge was built, it was reported to be the highest bridge in the state, at 250 feet above the river. It was listed in the National Register of Historic Places on July 16, 1982.

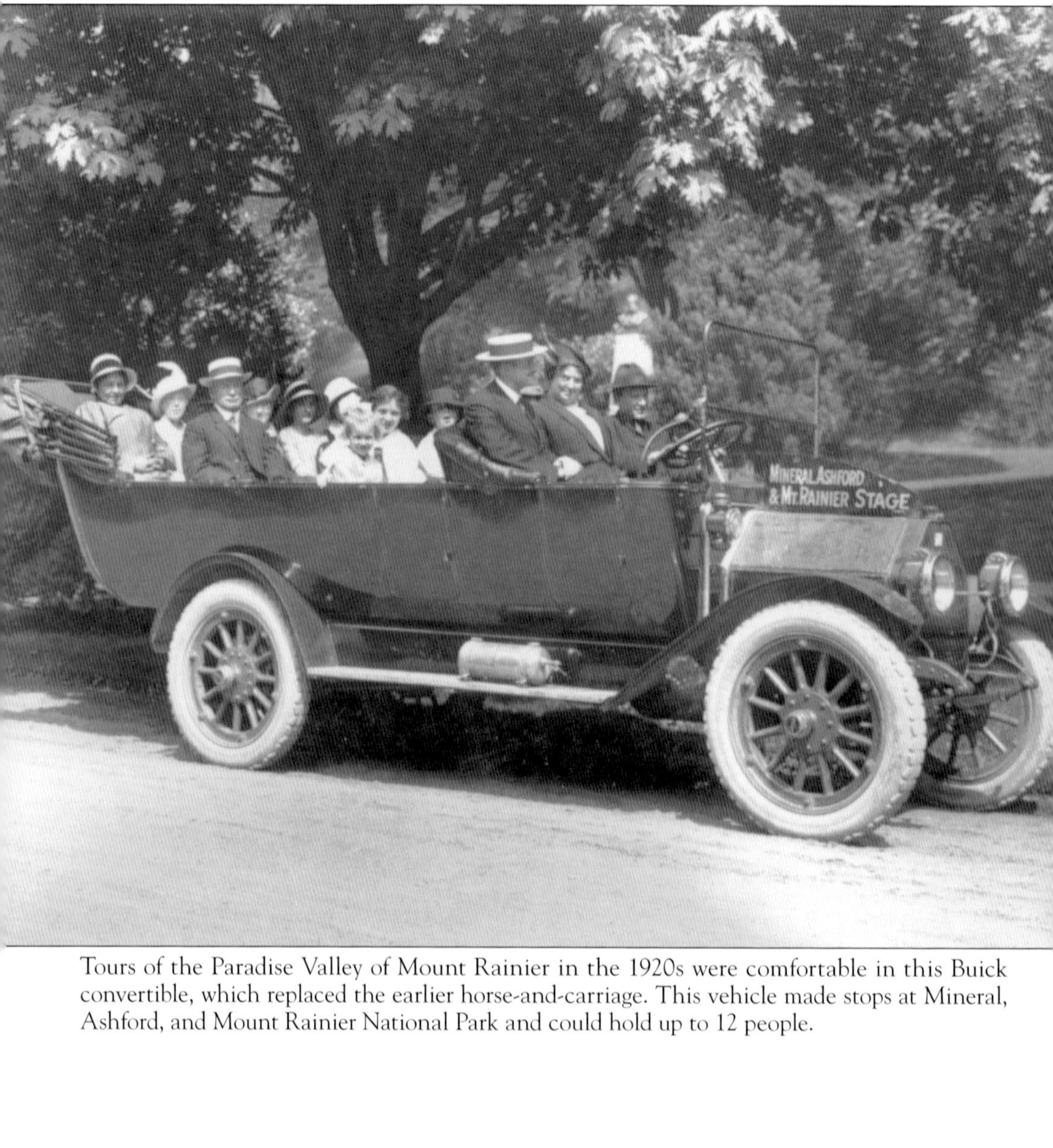


Tours of the Paradise Valley of Mount Rainier in the 1920s were comfortable in this Buick convertible, which replaced the earlier horse-and-carriage. This vehicle made stops at Mineral, Ashford, and Mount Rainier National Park and could hold up to 12 people.

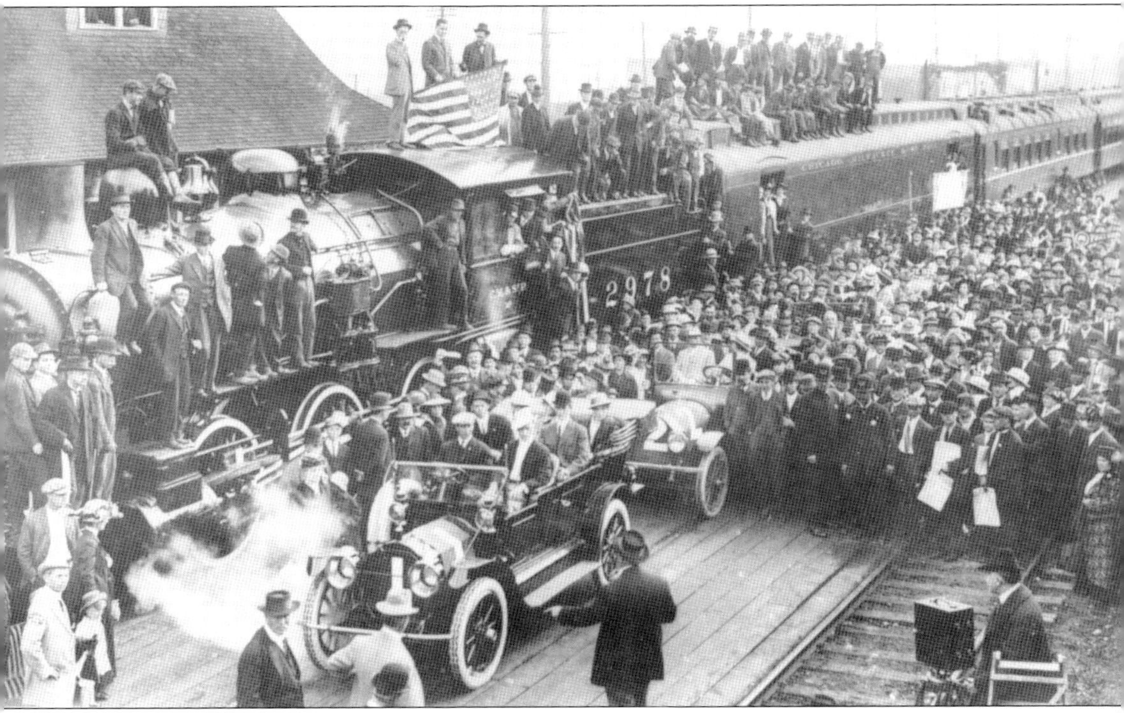


In the second car is Nadine E. Ridgeway, who won the Tacoma to the Mountain race sponsored by the Tacoma Publicity Committee on April 27, 1915. Thousands witnessed the race from Tacoma to Ashford.

The Paradise Lodge, Cafeteria, and Fountain at Mount Rainier was opened in June 1931 with 35 rooms and a lobby. In June 1965, it was purposely burned to the ground to make room for the Henry M. Jackson day-use center, which was itself purposely destroyed in 2009 to make room for the present day-use center, the Henry M. Jackson Memorial Visitor Center.

On April 12, 1930, at 6:00 p.m., a coal gas explosion killed 17 miners in a coal mine at Carbonado. The 17 miners were found about a mile from the mouth of the mine, 1,500 feet underground. Pictured here are, from left to right, H.A. Wilson, general manager of the coal company; George T. Wake, deputy state mine inspector; and William R. Reese, chief state mine inspector. No one in the area of the blast survived.

The Wilkeson Coal and Coke Company reopened the Skookum Slope coal mine, which had been closed since 1883, in March 1942. The mine was named after "Skookum" Smith, who participated in bringing the Northern Pacific Railway to Tacoma. This mine produced coal from March 1942 to November 1944, when it was closed once again. Only remnants of it remain today. The photograph below shows Munday Y. Loss at right with an unidentified miner hauling coal out of the Skookum Slope mine on March 13, 1944. The Wilkeson Coal and Coke Company had a contract with the US Defense Plant Corporation to produce coal for the war effort. This mine produced over 75,000 tons of coal before it was closed in November 1944.

Denver "Doc" Campbell is shown in this June 1, 1975, photograph greeting visitors to his carpentry shop in Carbonado. He was a 73-year-old carpenter and whittler, who got the name "Doc" because of his penchant for caring for sick animals. He had previously worked in West Virginia coal mines before coming to Carbonado but preferred woodworking in his later years.

Ezra Meeker was born on December 29, 1830, in Huntsville, Ohio, and settled with his family in the Northwest in 1887. He platted the city of Puyallup and gave it the name it has today. Meeker's 500 acres of hops eventually gave him the name "Hop King of the World." The city of Puyallup was incorporated in 1890 with Meeker being instrumental in the incorporation procedures. This photograph of Meeker was taken on September 14, 1926, the day his statue was dedicated at Pioneer Park in Puyallup, when he was 95 years old.

The Meeker Mansion was built around 1889 and is now in the Washington Heritage Register and the National Register of Historic Places. Meeker is credited with bringing electricity and water to the city of Puyallup in addition to retracing the Oregon Trail in 1906 in his preservation efforts. After being used as a hospital for some time, the Meeker Mansion was refurbished and opened to the public on March 20, 1998. It is presently open to visitors from March through November.

These coke ovens are part of the story of Pierce County's coal industry and of the boom time in "uptown" Wilkeson. The Tacoma Coal and Coke Company built the first 25 beehive coke ovens at Wilkeson in 1885. Coke was then shipped to ports as far as San Francisco and Alaska. Coke production reached a maximum of 125,872 tons in 1916, then declined steadily until production was terminated in 1937. The ovens are listed in the National Register of Historic Places, the Washington Heritage Register, and Pierce County Register of Historic Places, but are threatened with lack of protection from vandalism, neglect, and vegetation overgrowth.

In 1931, Pierce County formed the Community League, a nine-member baseball league that played a 16-game season. This ethnically diverse league featured this all-black team plus an all-Italian team headed by Al Greco, an all Japanese team from Fife, an all-Slavic team, the Tacoma Red Men, the 10th Field Artillery, Steilacoom, a Jack and Jill team, and a team from McKinley Hill. The team in this photograph was Monty's Independents, sponsored by Monty's Garage of Tacoma.

Climbers ascending Mount Rainier from Paradise Lodge, at an elevation of 5,420 feet, gain 4,680 feet by the time they reach Camp Muir at 10,000 feet. This trip normally takes five to six hours with a full pack ready to be taken to the summit the next day. The photograph below shows the preferred method of helicopter, which is used by some guides and suppliers of Camp Muir. Helicopters are also used on Mount Rainier in case a rescue is necessary. For searches and rescues at higher elevations, helicopters may have to be called in from Joint Base Lewis McChord. The shelters were built in 1916 and 1921 and listed in the National Register of Historic Places on March 13, 1991. (Both, author's collection.)

Janet Jones is looking up to her mother, Mrs. Kenneth Jones, who was the launching sponsor for the new US Navy YP-627, a self-propelled patrol craft that was launched on October 18, 1944, for the World War II effort. Western Boat Building Company constructed hundreds of vessels, including fishing, pleasure, and military craft, from 1916 through 1982.

George Lawler, a pioneer commercial bulb grower who came to Washington Territory at the age of two and settled in Pierce County in 1888, is shown with his great-grandchild in this photograph taken in 1936. In 1910, Lawler started his bulb farm with the purchase of five acres near Fife, which eventually became known as Gardenville in honor of all his flowers. As he eventually expanded his operation into growing bulbs, Lawler became one of the founders of the Northwest bulb industry. His bulb-growing operation eventually expanded to 383 acres near Roy, which were taken over during World War II for the Fort Lewis expansion.

These women are working in a shed at the George Lawler bulb farm in Gardenville, near Fife. They are "cleaning" the bulbs by hand, removing husks and separating the bulbs. Diseased or cut bulbs would be removed before grading and sizing.

The Washington State Fair, formerly called the Puyallup Fair, is the largest single attraction held annually in the state of Washington. It is one of the 10 largest fairs in the United States. The fair has two annual events: the 21-day Washington State Fair every September and the four-day Washington State Spring Fair every April. The facilities are available for rent for various events during the rest of the year, making the grounds a valuable community resource. A staff of 55 works year-round, and over 7,500 employees are hired each September during the fair.

Nole Floyd "Nokie" Edwards, of The Ventures fame, was the original lead guitarist for the group, which was founded in Tacoma in 1958. Edwards grew up in Puyallup from age five and, after a diverse and varied musical career, was inducted into the Rock & Roll Hall of Fame in 2008 along with the other members of the group. He passed away on March 12, 2018, in Yuma, Arizona.

The Elbe Church, still at its original location, was constructed in 1906. This small church, which is only 18 by 24 feet, with a 46-foot steeple, houses the original bell and Farrand and Votey bellows organ, which is still in use today. The church was listed in the National Register of Historic Places on October 8, 1976, and has been called America's smallest church by the Family Motor Coach Association. Church services and weddings are still held there. (Courtesy Benjamin Cody.)

Paradise Inn was built in 1916 at the 5,400-foot level of Mount Rainier and was listed in the National Register of Historic Places on May 28, 1987. The great hall is 50 feet by 112 feet and has a wraparound mezzanine. The dining room is 51 feet by 105 feet and has a 50-foot-high stone fireplace. In the great hall is a rustic piano that Pres. Harry S. Truman played in 1945 during a visit to the inn. (Courtesy Joe Mabel.)

McMillin Bridge, which is also known as the Puyallup River Bridge, does not get a lot of attention as being listed in the National Register of Historic Places, but it is. The bridge was designed by Homer M. Hadley, the same person who created the first floating bridge in Seattle, which opened to traffic in 1940. This concrete bridge was built in 1934 after Hadley had proposed the first Lake Washington floating bridge design, which was finally constructed in 1940. This bridge, which is no longer in use, has only two lanes that are 170 feet in length.

In May 1937, the Red Pig opened on the Tacoma-Seattle Highway, a half mile north of Fife. The original owner, Earl Smith, featured steak, chicken, and hamburgers with an "all-electric" kitchen when it opened.

Joe Fox, left, and his sister-in-law Bernice Fox are working behind the counter of the Red Pig in October 1938, soon after becoming the new owners. They had refitted and redecorated the roadside restaurant.

Narcisco Conception Rosario, pictured on September 2, 1962, owned and operated a 12-acre cucumber farm in Alderton, near Puyallup. He is shown here measuring a cucumber with a ring sizer. The Rosario farm supplied the ingredients for Farman pickles. Rosario was originally from the Philippines and moved to Washington in 1915. He moved to Pierce County from Yakima in 1959 and eventually passed away on November 6, 1983, at the age of 84.

Shown here are, from left to right, (seated) Janet Feldbush of Lakewood, Sue Smith of Lakewood, Linda Waters of Sumner, and Debbie Porter of Sumner; (standing) Dallas Dahle of Lakebay, Lyle McMillan of Puyallup, and Rick Nicolet of Everett. Cucumber pickers would normally pick between 300 pounds (for a beginner) and 600 pounds (for an efficient worker) a day and were paid 1¢ per pound in 1962.

These cottages are part of the Benbow Lakes Resort on the Mountain Highway between Tacoma and Mount Rainier. Benbow is a family resort made up of 500 acres and five lakes used for recreation and relaxation.

Benbow Lakes was the site of an American Red Cross Aquatic School for the Northwest, and the Red Cross Pierce County chapter held a 10-day water safety training school with 131 men and women from Washington, Oregon, Idaho, California, and Montana. There were only six such schools operated by the Red Cross in the United States when this photograph was taken in the summer of 1947. These students were being instructed in the then popular methods of artificial respiration.

This Willits canoe, built by Willits Brothers on Day Island in Tacoma, was being used during the summer American Red Cross Aquatic School, which took place at Benbow Lakes. Brothers Earl and Floyd Willits built less than 1,000 canoes on Day Island from 1905 to 1962.

# *Five*

# West

## McNeil Island, Gig Harbor, Longbranch, and Vaughn

Shown here from left to right are Robert Troutman, John Drake, Gilbert L. Palmer (warden), John Devoin, Robert Longmire (deputy warden), Frank Mooney, and H.E. Palmer standing next to Cell House No. 1 on McNeil Island around 1900. The brick and stone building, completed in 1874, had 48 double cells. McNeil Island territorial prison opened on May 28, 1875, and was a federal penitentiary until 1976. From 1981 until 2011, it housed the McNeil Island Corrections Center. It is now abandoned except for a detention center for violent sexual offenders.

This is a c. 1900 chain gang at the McNeill Island Federal Penitentiary. Prisoners at that time worked in the fields, cleared and farmed the land, and prepared it for gardens. Prisoners usually wore the striped uniforms provided by the prison or occasionally their own clothes while working in the fields. The guards are shown in dark suit-like uniforms. At this time, some women were prisoners on McNeil Island, but they worked in the guard's quarters doing mostly domestic chores.

McNeil Island was named after William Henry McNeill, a boat captain for the Hudson's Bay Company and founder of Victoria, British Columbia. Ezra Meeker homesteaded the island in 1853 before the federal government purchased 27 acres in 1870 to build the territorial prison. The government purchased the entire island in 1937, and all homesteaders were forced to leave. This photograph was taken in 1956 as the ferryboat to the island approached the dock.

This is a view on the Key Peninsula from Vaughn Cemetery overlooking Vaughn Bay. The flags are in place for the annual Memorial Day ceremonies. (Author's collection.)

The Washington Cooperative Association was very active in western Washington prior to the Depression. This is what the Gig Harbor plant looked like on September 9, 1928. The mosquito fleet was a very important part of getting eggs and poultry to market for the farmers in the area.

This island was previously called Graves Island since it was an early burial ground for Native Americans. It was bought in 1933 by Dr. Alfred L. Schultz, renamed Tanglewood Island in 1947, and run as a boy's camp called Ta-Ha-Do-Wa. According to Schultz, the Smithsonian Institute had removed all traceable relics from Grave Island prior to 1891. The lighthouse and pavilion were eventually demolished on January 24, 2014, after many years of neglect.

Mitchell Skansie is shown with his family at their home in Gig Harbor around 1908. At this time, he was about 28 years old and was part of the Skansie brothers fishing and boatbuilding family, which included his brothers Peter, Joe, and Andrew. The family boatyard produced fishing boats and ferries that were always durable and well-built. Mitchell Skansie later operated the Washington Navigation Company, which controlled most of the ferries in Pierce County.

Workmen at Skansie's Ship Building Co. in Gig Harbor took time out to pose for this photograph showing the progress of the 180-foot wooden ferry *Defiance*. This ferry made her first run from Gig Harbor to Tacoma on April 3, 1927, and had the capacity to carry 70 cars. To the left of *Defiance* is the ferry boat *City of Steilacoom*, which was nearing completion.

On November 12, 1926, the ferry *Wollochet* was docked at Skansie's Ship Building Co. It had been launched by the Gig Harbor firm the previous year and was in service at this time.

On the ferry *Skansonia*, in July 1931, commuters between Point Defiance and Gig Harbor could sit on one of these stools and order a fried ham sandwich for 15¢. A Swiss cheese sandwich, hamburger, or hot dog were only 10¢. *Skansonia* was built at Skansie's Ship Building Co. in 1929.

Wilbur Dukes and Allison Moore are shown paddling their canoe near Eagle Island between McNeill Island and Anderson Island, with Mount Rainier in the background. The south end of Puget Sound is sometimes called the "bathtub of the Salish Sea" because it normally is very calm and does not have the swift currents that are found elsewhere. (Author's collection.)

In August 1926, these two Mack trucks were parked at a wooded site in Gig Harbor as they were being used to clear land. Barlow and Sons, an old Tacoma firm established in 1882, was the owner of these trucks.

In Gig Harbor, the Tides Tavern, previously the West Side Grocery, is shown with the *Florence K*, a passenger steamer built by Crawford & Reid of Tacoma in 1903, docked alongside. The Skansie brothers' shipyard is to the right. *Florence K* would later serve as the ferry *Beeline* until it was taken over by the US Navy during World War II and likely scrapped following the war.

In August 1926, Killian Van R. Schermerhorn, standing, and Wilmot McCune rowed from Point Defiance to Olympia and back. These two Stadium High School adventurers rented their boat from the park's boathouse for this 80-nautical-mile trip, where they hopped from island to island and camped along the way. Their excursion took them a week and even included an overnight stay on McNeil island, after they convinced the guards they were not trying to assist anyone with an escape plan.

Gov. Dixy Lee Ray is smiling at Paul Meyers on December 9, 1980, as she is being introduced as a guest speaker. Meyers was a retired Great Northern Railway agent, and Ray was the Democratic governor of Washington in 1976, serving one term as Washington's first female governor. She retired to her home on Fox Island and passed away on January 2, 1994, at the age of 79.

On September 17, 1947, at the Western Washington Fair in Puyallup, Tacoma mayor Val Fawcett is shown with his granddaughters viewing prize flowers. Linda Knecht is at left, and Mary Claire Petrich is at right holding a small trophy.

The granary, which was originally at Fort Steilacoom and later moved to Fort Nisqually at Point Defiance, can legitimately be considered the oldest standing structure in the Puget Sound area. Records show that the granary's construction took place between July 1850 and January 1851. Today, this historic structure is an integral part of Fort Nisqually's education and interpretation program as well as a designated national historic landmark. This photograph was taken on February 25, 1945.

Camp Seymour, a very popular boy's camp at Glen Cove on the Key Peninsula, was the destination for these boys on August 2, 1924. The Tacoma Rotary Club sponsored 60 boys so they could experience a week at camp, which included swimming, camping, Bible study, and a lot of group experiences. They are in front of the YMCA building at 714 Market Street waiting for the bus to leave for camp.

Born in Seattle on September 6, 1897, Wendell Corwin Chase was a mountaineer, woodsman, poet, author, and philosopher and was known for his woodblock prints. This photograph was taken on January 6, 1963, as he was displaying his works at the Handforth Gallery in the Tacoma Public Library. Chase's artwork has been featured at auction and in galleries throughout the United States and still appears when available to this day. He lived in Vaughn, Washington, until his death on December 24, 1988.

On July 1, 1940, there were over 60 floats entered in a parade to commemorate the opening of the first Tacoma Narrows Bridge. The message on the float reads, "The Peninsula. Playground of the Northwest. Gig Harbor." This was a standard marketing theme for both Gig Harbor and the Key Peninsula, even after the second bridge was completed and in use.

This c. 1912 photograph shows the Skansie brothers' shipyard in Gig Harbor. Four Yugoslavian brothers, Pete, Mitchell, Andrew, and Joe Skansie, started this shipyard in 1912. They were the leading builders of ferries and fishing boats in Pierce County for many years.

The ferry *Skansonia* is returning to Tacoma from Camp Seymour on the Key Peninsula. A group of newspaper boys is on the upper deck as the boat is beginning to dock. They had earned a trip to Camp Seymour as an incentive for their sales and delivery activities. Launched on August 24, 1929, the *Skansonia*, built by the Skansie Ship Building Co., was 165 feet in length and could carry 65 automobiles and 500 passengers.

The Point Defiance Pagoda was built in 1914, and this photograph was taken on February 8, 1923. The pagoda was used as a streetcar station until 1938, when vehicles could be driven into Point Defiance with regularity. It was restored in the mid-1980s and is now rented out for weddings, receptions, banquets, and family gatherings by Tacoma Metroparks.

Emmett Hunt and his brothers built the steamer *Atalanta*, shown in this c. 1914 photograph shortly after it was built in 1913. The *Atalanta* is said to have the distinction of being the last passenger steamer on the Tacoma–Gig Harbor route and at the same time to be the first to carry cars in the pre-ferry era, when cars were hoisted onto the boat like cargo. She was 112 feet long and cruised at 16 knots.

This photograph was taken from the Gig Harbor side for the opening of the Narrows Bridge on July 1, 1940. Adm. Edward B. Fenner, the Bremerton Navy Yard commandant, is cutting the ribbon. To his left is Mayor Homer Jones, of Bremerton, and to his right is John Schlarb, chairman of the Pierce County Board of Commissioners. The City of Gig Harbor was not incorporated until July 12, 1946, so it had no official representative for this ceremony.

Oscar H. Swanson is shown next to trophies and a display of eggs on September 9, 1928, at the Gig Harbor Fair. He was the founder of the Gig Harbor Washington Co-operative Association. At the time this photograph was taken, eggs and poultry were major businesses in the Gig Harbor area.

These dedicated Key Peninsula Historical Society and Museum volunteers are presently working to bring the Vaughn Library Hall back to life for its original use. From left to right are Ron Kingsbury, Paul Michaels, Frank Shirley, Ron Schillinger, Barton Wolfe, Frank Slater, and Diane Jackman. (Photograph by Jacqueline "Jacquie" Hickey; courtesy Barton Wolfe.)

This photograph of the Vaughn Library Hall shows how it appeared as this book was being written. Progress has been made on the restoration since that time and the long-range plan by the Key Peninsula Historical Society and Museum is to make it appear as it did during its prime. The Vaughn Library Hall was originally started in 1889 and served as a community center, library, church, and personal residence throughout its history.

Three geoduck diggers are showing off their catch at the Department of Natural Resources public area at the south end of the Longbranch Peninsula, near Devil's Head. Geoducks are considered a delicacy in some parts of the world and are dug by many in the south Puget Sound area when the tides are low. (Author's collection.)

The Lakebay Marina Resort was placed in the Pierce County Register of Historical Places on February 12, 2019, and the Washington Heritage Register as the Washington Co-operative Egg & Poultry Association–Lakebay Station on June 28, 2019. It is presently in operation and in the process of restoration and upgrading to serve south Puget Sound boaters with mooring, a restaurant, and a place to fill up with gas.

On December 10, 1921, shortly before the first paved county road came through, the Longbranch Improvement Club was incorporated to "purchase real estate for recreation and for a consolidated school." The building in this photograph, which was constructed in 1938, was listed in the National Register of Historic Places on September 28, 1987.

On August 21, 2017, parts of the western United States were treated to an almost complete eclipse of the sun. The residents of the Taylor Bay Beach Club near Longbranch gathered with their protective eyeglasses and folding chairs to view the spectacle. (Author's collection.)

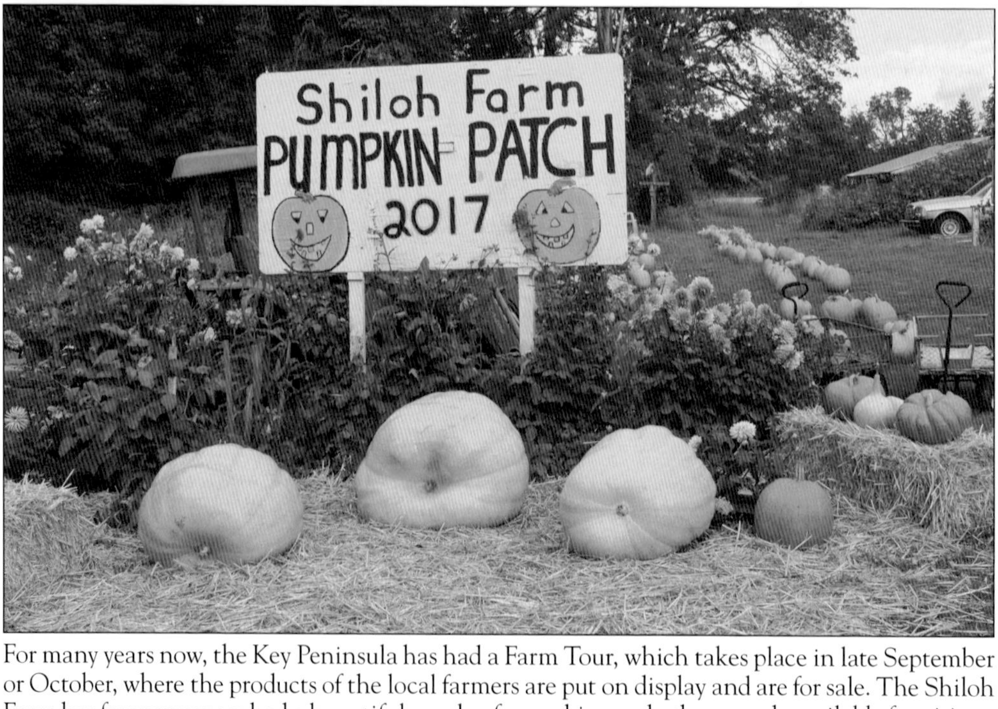


For many years now, the Key Peninsula has had a Farm Tour, which takes place in late September or October, where the products of the local farmers are put on display and are for sale. The Shiloh Farm has for many years had a bountiful supply of pumpkins and other gourds available for visitors during this season. (Author's collection.)

# Bibliography


Arledge, R.T. *Early Days of the Key Peninsula*. Vaughn, WA: Key Peninsula Historical Society, 1998.

Bancroft, Hubert Howe. *History of Washington, Idaho, and Montana 1845–1889*. San Francisco, CA: The History Company, 1890.

Harvey, Paul W. *Tacoma Headlines*. Tacoma, WA: *Tacoma News Tribune*, 1962.

Hawthorne, Julian. *History of Washington the Evergreen State*. New York, NY: American Historical Publishing Co., 1893.

Heritage League of Pierce County. *A History of Pierce County Washington 1990*. Dallas, TX: Taylor Publishing Company, 1990.

Hunt, Herbert, and Floyd C. Kaylor. *Washington West of the Cascades*. Chicago, IL: S.J. Clarke Publishing Company, 1917.

Jepsen, David J., and David J. Norberg. *Contested Boundaries*. Hoboken, NJ: Wiley Blackwell, 2017.

Pierce County. Survey & Inventory of Historic Properties. Tacoma, WA: Artifacts Architectural Consulting, 2010.

Pierce County Pioneer Association. *Commemorative Celebration at Sequalitchew Lake, Pierce County Washington, July 5, 1906*. Tacoma, WA: Vaughan and Morrill Printing, 1906.

Prosch, Thomas W. *McCarver and Tacoma*. Seattle, WA: Lowman & Hanford Stationery and Printing Company, 1906.

Tacoma Chamber of Commerce. *Tacoma Illustrated*. Chicago, IL: Baldwin, Calcutt & Co. 1889.

Traver, George W. *Tacoma and Vicinity*. Tacoma, Washington Territory: George W. Traver, 1889.

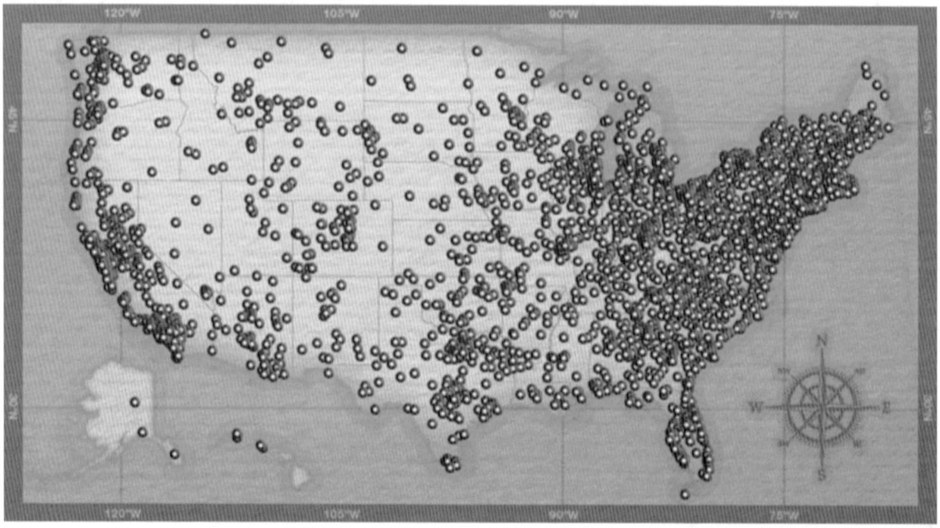